THERE'S COMFORT IN THE DARKNESS
© 2016 by Justin Sky
http://www.justinsky.com

Over The Edge Books, Los Angeles, CA
overtheedgebooks.com

ISBN 9781944082239
ISBN 978xxxxxxxxxxelectronic
First Edition

All rights reserved. No part of this book may be reproduced or transmitted in any form or by any means, electronic or mechanical, including photocopying, recording, or by information storage and retrieval systems, without the written permission of the publisher, except by a reviewer who may quote brief passages in a review.

Printed in the United States of America

this book is for Noah Jai

Who stood at the precipice of death and simply smiled. Who taught me how to exist. Who taught me how to love. Who has the sweetest smile in all the lands. Who loves his sister. Who has the heart of God within.

Who is "strong like Spiderman."

Who asked "Why are you crying?"

I still ponder that question. I still search for you in everything. I love you. You are beyond. You are ascended. If I am to be anything of value in this dimension, it is because of you. Everything I create is for you, and in remembrance of you. These words could never be enough. Ever. So, here's my life.

Things get dark.

But you taught me to find comfort there.

I love you forever.

this book is for Nyah Kamil

Who is unwavering in her love. Who is the most insightful person I've ever met. Who understands the deepest thing in the universe: love. Who has the heart of God within. Who has been through the unspeakable and walked out holding light in her hands. Who flies with me on journeys beyond comprehension. Often. Who constantly pushes me to be better. Who loves her brother. Who is constantly assessing her purpose. You are the epitome. There is no follow up to that. You are just the epitome. You teach me how to live. These words could never be enough. So, here is my life. I love you "beyond the stars and all the way to the galaxies". And back. Forever.

THERE'S COMFORT IN THE DARKNESS

Justin Sky

"night"

i'll bathe myself in placid thought
til dawn is drawn and night's forgot
til seas of doubt have long been dry
and oceans filled with sun draw nigh
when moons have set their feet upon
the weary road of which i'm on
i hide my eyes from the beneath
in hopes the night won't show it's teeth

"time, the omni"

beneath the fabric of our worlds
are woven winding trees
the roots of which know not an end
beyond the astral seas

humanity lies but a speck
a drop amongst the deep
it runs so swiftly far and wide
but never moves its feet

our lives inhale, but at its whim
a mist amongst the storm
each moment but a memory
forgotten and forlorn

to value does not justice do
its rareness not compared
submerge into its vastness now
ascend its winding stair

"ending"

A tide of tears to drown the pain
the water knows me well
below my fears the blood will stain
and in this fate I dwell

"!"

Aiming for the sky!
Headed to another galaxy!
Feelings never die!
Imma take you for a ride!
Be ready for this traveling!
Baby you and I!

"finding out"

placid thoughts
lucid dreams
relax in fault
move with streams
current-forsaker, currently forsaken
forgotten forever in folly, it seems.

"ode to lonely"

found you amongst the ghosts and blunder
a folly few forgot
i pr(e)y that you become the hunter
unweave secluded knot

your shadow spills on sacred sun
your pulse a growing glow
i'll purge you from my lover's tongue
on tranquil river's row

you kept an eye, a thoughtful eye
upon my muddled dance
too long beneath my roots you drank
through life's untimely chance

i know too well your countenance
your silhouette's eclipse
and bid you never speak again
through sorrow's softest lips

"run"

i don't know why it runs from me
i've waited four score at its door
like the waves on shores of forgotten cliffs
i haven't fallen, but i've slipped
asking questions like
what's truth?
and
why do grey areas breed hungry wolves?
carnivores in kind with sharp tooth
i wish it be done
i've bled in every.single.capsule
every needle tastes like death on my tongue
grave's gauntlets and guillotine dreams flew
through my consciousness like owls on the hunt
running from morning dew like moon
rays afraid of impending doom
i've bled in every.single.corner
of the house they built to keep me in
three feet from the lion's den
torso out and two feet in

kickin off my killers with soles full of soul
i'd never admit it was my fault though...
i mean...
i don't have the power to make the sun gleam and
configure countless quantum trajectories
of trillions of human lives
and random occurrences
keep planets in the sky
just a guy
trying to find the balance between
responsible and responsive
control and subconscious
will power and wind power
did i choose ease if the breeze is my easel?
can i paint a masterpiece if the Master's peace
seems evil?
i've bled on every.single.paintbrush
and somehow the burgundies turned rose
so i'll chase after it until my skin is some par-
ticle
flying through the heavens like the tail end of a
super hero's cape
caught in the night wind
i'll run til i end.

"higher water"

find peace between the crashing waves
the current pulls us in
beneath the skies, I've found my place
the water calls me kin

"infinite autumn"

our souls so leaf eternal fall
an autumn in the deep
we've held the sky
the land
the drops
now follow swift upstream

"endless travel"

travel with sand-covered sandals
riding these camels to stars simmering
candles and lamps flickering
damp taverns, eyes glistening

bewildered in wilderness, beasts bickering
stiff sleep & trembling, dripping
teeth shimmering underneath sheets of
crippling fear, defeat

remembering images of pillaged villages
unfinished sentences and brims unfulfilled
militant diligent foes diggin for gold
on religious roads

finger-made quilts built to linger on stiff stilts
still as the set of the sun's lingering tilt
demeanor of guilt felt on feeling the thrill
of...
traveling with sand-covered sandals...

"a.i."

these strands of mind and sacred thought
have spilled between crevasse forgot
a narrow hall of broken dreams
humanity, so blind, it seems.

.

"naked created"

with only her breath to keep me warm,
i face the frozen with my skin.
her heart paced my steps while our silhouettes
cast giants against the tower.
winter isn't welcoming to naked bodies,
and neither was i.
"look",
she whispered briskly,
gesturing towards an opening in a tree-lined crev-
ice.

i never thought i'd be this vulnerable.

but her confidence was strangely magnetic.
we continued to tread heavily
through the porcelain colored snow
our bareness screaming louder
and more commanding in my ear.
pain. regret.
at the same time, i drew more and more anxious.

hungry to see where our
freedom would lead us.
i drew back the branches and brushed the
shimmering icicles from her skin.
they reminded me of the skyline I fell asleep to
back home.
the purest of radiance.
far...

i held her hand as she reached for the door and
pushed it open.
it never felt so perfectly safe to be
naked and afraid.

"my love"

what do I love?
if not the forest,
the trees that sever the sunlight.

"showtime"

when I feel,
it's not because I choose to.
solitude summons visions of a cold,
but rapidly growing treasure beneath my seas of
uncertainty.
curtains remain tangled and servants to the stage,
but at the close of the show, who will stay?
close my eyes
and the lack of darkness frightens me.
luminary clues to my new existence exude.
and I find myself falling forever.
act iii: intermission.

"flight"

a cliffside farewell heeds a troublesome warning,
as our protagonist fears he may never feel the cold,
sentient comfort of the ground ever again.
scarred.
fade to grey.
[end scene]

"reality's remorse"

i took a dive inside your eyes
my breath can wait it's turn
contort your tempest, bend your rain
to fall on ashes burned

cascade your life in heart so empty
drown my sacred cup
a spill from you allows me to
ascend our souls to much

no absolutes, no end in sight
untold travels we shape
to hold incessant bliss in hand
and nether-worlds create

the gods do envy you and i
we've broken cosmic course
to form a love so far beyond
reality's remorse

"flight, ep 2: fight"

dim lights.
our hero emerges from the water and debris.
unscathed. determined. angry.
lights.
the beast can sense it's own demise.
run.

"kinda sad right now"

an island of my pain
an ocean of my tears
the waterfall
the rain
my soul won't disappear

"curse-iv"

there's a land that exists
in the outskirts of abyss
where oblivion is king
and the frozen shadows sing

where the truth is not obscure
and the lies hold title pure
under forests filled of moons
wrapped in life's impending doom

you will find him floating there
among the great despair
it is he who holds the key
to chasm built of peace

"focus"

in all the sights my eyes embraced
within the light of day
it is the night in which i stay
the moon to light the way

"deafinite"

smooth brush strokes stir color onto my canvas
i wonder of musical wanderlust
and journeys for answers
i can't hear my name
nor her cries for help
nor the gunshots behind me
nor life itself
sonically betrayed by the harmonies conveyed
ink joining tears with the pain on this page

"the wind dash why"

steps towards the ethereal mist
my thoughts a cliff to fall
i move through solemn and tighten my fists
but you unravel them all

"j"

what wayward wants doth break our hearts?
that sun and moon keep us apart
on mile
on league
on time
on space
will bring us once back to our place

"exit"

one day you'll look and i'll be gone
but when day comes, please do not mourn
i tried, i reached to take your hand
to join the journey i am on

"drift"

drift with me girl, beyond the moons
through starry streams of love
reflect our place on waters deep
our souls ascend above

run with me, love, we'll pass the sun
adrift on oceans far
your hazel eyes will light our skies
and i'll keep you from harm

to worlds unknown, we've come, we've flown
just promise that you'll stay
we'll take our flight til day is night
and night becomes the day

and when we wake on heaven's lake
too far to head back home
we'll build our place through time and space
the galaxy our throne

"kamil"

when thousand suns can warm no more
and placid sands hold not a shore
a comfort in my thoughts reprise
to look upon your graceful eyes

"amidala the phoenix"

painted by the gods in skies
the strokes evoke your hue
a thousand times inside your eyes
i've made my promise too

calligraphy on calloused hands
a labor not in vain
to break the bounds of art profound
the angels scribe your name

i fell asleep inside your keep
dimensions dim the light
for all do not deserve to see
or hold you in their sight

i'll swim within your sacred sea
nirvana claims her own
to float adrift, to live, to be
in solace yet unknown

"who am i v1"

mirrors tell the story
of an ancient tomorrow
where the present is a lie
and my image is borrowed
do my eyes deceive?
or is this really me?
must look past the pain and the anger to see

"i'm not crazy, i'm free"

pain resides in the eyes
but camouflage in my demeanor
i'm an open book
and by the looks
still a mirror to the reader

"promises"

i never left
you said you'd stay
beyond the mist
within the grey

"transitions"

into the depths all paths do lead
beyond the starry gaze
the subtle cry of falling leaves
the dark
beneath
the waves

"give and take. the phoenix"

entangled minds and thoughts so 'twined
we've held our hands and danced
through scopes of hope 'cross devil's trope
and heaven's fleeting stance

across the hills of sorrow's spill
beyond our morals' grasp
and kissed the lips of lives amidst
a fiction's time and chance

if i could stay, i'd lay all day
in solitude with you
and sculpt anew to question truth
and paint the dawn your hue

my soul is stirred through tales unheard
our minds to yet reveal
let's kiss beneath the fallen leaf
that tree's forbidden yield

"strength"

spilled theories on the edges of certainty
blood stained on my hands
upon faintest glimpse i place my fate
and on the waves i
stand

"taking the light"

upon the shadows lay fair skin
a bliss i've never known
the sun does row upon her water
and make her face its home

i'm raptured in her countenance
a soul for sol's revel
though i'd kill the light for you
and in your prison dwell

but can i taste your silhouette
if lumens never speak?
i've come a quandary far to win
as sun embraced your cheek

if i could, i'd steal the sun
i'm jealous, i admit
for i can't be what gives you life
and on your beauty sit

"patience"

escape the sure fate of the river
do not fall[acy]
instead, pursue the peak as a lion to the sheep
truth only waits if she
loves you

"inhale"

if you find her
drown in her morning star
the light take life but birth you new
breath returns on morning dew

"alchemy"

creating with broken pieces
sculpting with hopeless feelings
crafting a masterpiece
alchemy got feet on throats of demons
who feeds on the thrones of kings?
with leaves sewn for wings
a gavel rattles his feet
from belly of beast he sings
saw him in a dream
i awaken painting his eulogy
taking shades of his blues
using his muse as energy
saving for the future
so i'm inspired posthumously
now my piece of art is peace at heart
twists of the unknown
can lead a blind man's flight
and bring the lost ones home

"smh"

let her know my insides are rioting
rotting away like a corpse rotten
the irony
is that i love when she lie to me
tell me you don't love me

hey. you are about midway through this book, but i was just thinking...
although our lives are extremely influenced and altered by the actions of others,
there's a certain amount of control we have over ours...
the key is to understand the balance between letting life happen and MAKING life happen.
when people say you're totally in control, they're merely trying to comfort themselves.
"there's no comfort in the truth."
but, one cannot grow from a comfort zone.
life cannot happen. life without growth is death.
life requires uncomfortable circumstances.
how will we know when to make things happen and when to let things happen?
discernment. wisdom. study patterns in your life and the life around you. prayer. meditation. focus and pay attention to surroundings.
then you will know. because we're so influenced by the actions of others, what is going on around you is vital.

this is why it is very important to understand and attempt a level of control over who you surround yourself with.
those around you can tell you a lot about where you're going or where you are in life.
life is about balance. balance balance balance.
because of the fact that we perceive things differently,
well-rounded lives benefit us most.
exert a balance of movement in your life.
the ocean is a wonderful example.
the sea has such power, yet such grace. storms. calm. ripples. waves. burning hot temperatures, and freezing. all to sustain life on earth.
a wise man once told me that a wise Indian man once said that a wise man told him that knowledge was "your relationship with nature".
if nature is what is happening around us without our influence, then knowledge is learning how to move WITH....

in the year 2000, an amazing artist said
"i wanna know how you move,
i wanna know so i can move too"
wisdom.
how does nature move? how does God move? how does the universe move? ... move too...
exert this balance in every aspect of life and see how you move... like it or not, you are never fully in control.
and that's ok. do you what you can. do it when it's right.
timing is more powerful than action.
the unknown will work itself out.

"who am i v2"

who love i?
no speak
no hear
but who stop i?
no greed
no fear
now you watch i
obstacles disappear
and crescendos of victory rising high in my ear

"origins"

origins are pouring in to feed my
eternal
hunger
i meditate in lucid state
to pull myself from
slumber
dark doors
light steps
tall forest, a fright kept
fear of the unknown
comfort in oblivion
absence is mirage
my eyes have seen the end

"the end"

it all must come to end, I know
a truth of no escape
the ash of trees, no sun to glow
the mist from barren lake

the dust of ground, once human flesh
the silence in the dark
was once crescendo great and wide
the stillness of the heart

and in this lies the fondest dream
the warmth of the beneath
for in the end maybe there's peace
inside the gallow's keep

so at this door, i wait, i pray
to enter within time
my body need only follow
i'm there within my mind

"alone"

time is lost
unseen mist
the distance between
the crescendo and the cliff
fall or love
the difference is this:
wind won't carry my innocence

"language"

when it's really felt
you don't have to say
but words remind my heart
not to float away

"untitled"

my thoughts bleed for the placid
a peace drowned in acid
wings of my passion in a sea of tainted actions
what is life, but a memory...

"eyes"

my eyes, sometimes they lie to me
they sketch a world untrue
alas, in time, they show me real
when i should gaze at you

"shores of the phoenix"

at bottom of the darkest deep
i lie in wait and pain
for light to call in song with me
for your flow in my vein

my body knows a sacred lie
it's bled into my brain
my mind a constant waveless beach
and you the sand that stays

and as i drown, i see your face
to pull me to the sky
you've lifted every morsel of
my darkened placid life

you the altar on which i pray
my temple made in stone
forever on your field I graze
your spirit I call home

"golden"

if there were none left
but her eyes and her voice,
i would die a thousand lives
and place harmonies on her delicate soul
i say she gold

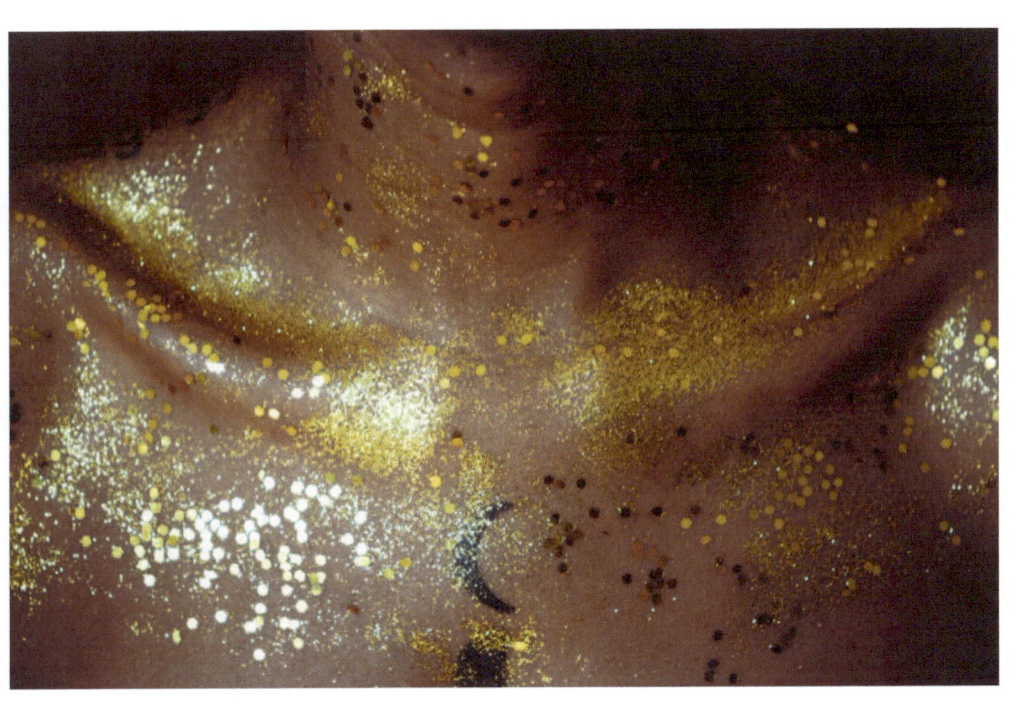

"currency"

i traded in my gold bars for a pair of wings
my sharpened scissors for
a spaceship through the seams
exchange rate between the gold and my soul
vs the netherlife never ceases to unfold
the creases do unfold
the demons go untold
in a tale of fallen old
torn souls go un-sowed
but the story of the rise
is always read between the lies

"who am i v3"

i took their hatred to the lake
and held it under the water
my first murder addictive
i make love to the slaughter

"still"

the air is still and the night is fallen
the wind has made its home
the waters whisper, the moon is solemn
yet my true love has grown

i pull the knife, i've bled, it's true
through carousels of pain
i place a coin to ride again
embrace the acid rain

volcanoes cry with fire's eyes
and asteroids do fall
like teardrops down my tortured skies
but she shan't weep at all

i've made my home within the storm
i promised not to run
so if it be, i'll bleed in peace
eternities to come

"untitled 2"

great distance,
sea depths
hold the inhale
breathe yet,
still must be still
touched my window
rock thrown
so i caught it before i'm boxed bones
defeat risks, meet cliffs
i don't want to land

"daphne"

sights set on suns not yet set
dawn holds my heart in its linger
the song
my physical at peace
soul ascending to escape its net
your melody
the singer

"heart problems"

trapped on my lips
longing for the free
relapse by a drift
lean towards the flee
conundrum
constant flight
cast for lead in the plight of we

"man, i really loved this girl"

i'm all over
spilled in slow of my still let go
no pieces to pick
no
reason to stick
in reverse it's as deep as the sea of my sick

"live twice"

rest be to the Lazarus Few
in depth, we came in peace
down from above, yet set below
mortality's defeat

"lost"

wrapped in wilderness
ghosts and resonance
of
...
living in now never hurt so
rain clouds embrace my vertigo

"qm"

when studying
the space time continuum
i realized that you are
and all the way across those
millions of
light years
it wouldn't have changed

"phoenix. the beginning."

the wind rattled against the eyes of the river,
pushing its gaze towards the forest.
a pale moonlight kept a steady glow and open arms
for him to embrace.
he landed by the bank of the river...
slowly...
ashes on his hands and stardust on his feet.
as he used the crisp, cool water to cleanse his
face and fingers,
he could hear the ever-present voices
in the distance...
louder and
louder.
tears mixed with the river's elixir, as he bathed
one last time...
she would not be forgotten.

"hidden"

suppression
in hopes it's not digression
i hide
implosion is imminent if change won't reside
you know
yet still
i don't understand

"i beg of you"

leave me be in misery
myself crawls out
hesitantly
a peasant and a queen
will never convene
deliver from river
dry my ravine
please

"tower of wounds"

upon plateau of broken hearts
a sight no more to man
the peace of death has reached its rest
eternity at hand

above our temples, waters flow
the air is but a dream
but let us drown and take our place
under the shadow's wing

to look no more upon the mast
the monolith a sign
that all the woes of many men
will breed our path to find

the isle an aisle and eye for eye
to see what's really there
an eon of forgetfulness
true life without a care

"who am i fin"

now mirror do dance
she conjuring rain
she know who i am
but call me insane
she be enemy but i love her the same
my vision beside me
she numbing the pain

"quandary"

i'm still good at the other stuff
mystique
teach me, i'm gifted
one eye on the lifted
sleep's cousin encrypted
may just
forget it

"sg"

hate is such a strong word
the way you are a songbird
that sounded better in my head
like us

"sg2"

lunar rendezvous
after the sun
before the two
telepathic attempts
not content
with anything less than next to you

"ascend"

hey,
i know you are nearing the end of this book,
but i just wanted to share some thoughts with you:

when you are fearful of your belonging and purpose,
remember that every single human ever questioned
their place.
you are not alone.
surround yourself with those that feed you love,
challenge you, and want nothing more than you to
ascend through life.
genuine people are out there. we've just got to be
open. they aren't perfect, but surrounding yourself
with them will literally save your life.
simply connecting with another person can change
the way you view life. it can save people from depression, anxiety, and inadequacy...
just knowing that there is someone else in this
world that feels what you're going through is
priceless.

other people are the most important thing in the universe. how we treat people and make them feel matters most.
so, emit love. you never know who is on the brink of collapsing and may need YOU.

"song"

the longest wait across the stars
a melody in time
in every note i place my hope
for love's return to find

"phoenix ascending, a story of love"

the ancient gods, spirits of old
have conquered worlds unknown
orchestral muses bathe in gold
and all to taste your tone

a cherub's whisper's no compare
and queens in time have sought
to hold a candle to your gaze
for your hand, wars were fought

you rise now from beneath my dreams
and i'll FOREVER wait
to look upon your wondrous wings
your fire tempts my fate

my breath is still, unwavered eyes
the atmosphere within
i've peered into a love beyond
engulfed but at your whim

and as I lay, my thoughts so free
to wander skies so true
my Phoenix now, i'll sacrifice
my life to be with you

"truth"

why hide your face? why weave a tale
so fleeting at its core?
i've searched for you and left my hue
upon your painting's floor

all men have tried to taste your thoughts
some claim their fellowship
but woe to he who boasts your soul
all life upon your lips

i envy you! your constant ways
my mind a steadfast sway
but stone holds not a candle to
your everlasting gaze

since atom's dawn you danced along
horizon's far to see
that you reveal the all too real
and you shall set us free

"interview with a deity"

what solemn fate beneath us waits
towards tombs and shadows, sun's escape
when once we see our likeness gleam
too heavy on our human's dream

for solitude and open wound
for timeless lies in frozen tomb
we seek our paths upon the sand
and let not higher have its hand

but when sun sets we seek not shade
for life and death have not been made
to fault our hearts and what they seek
our eyes, our vision, yet beneath

to know not what we do not know
and toil and tear in blindness go
to ends beyond our thoughts compare
there's comfort in the darkness there.

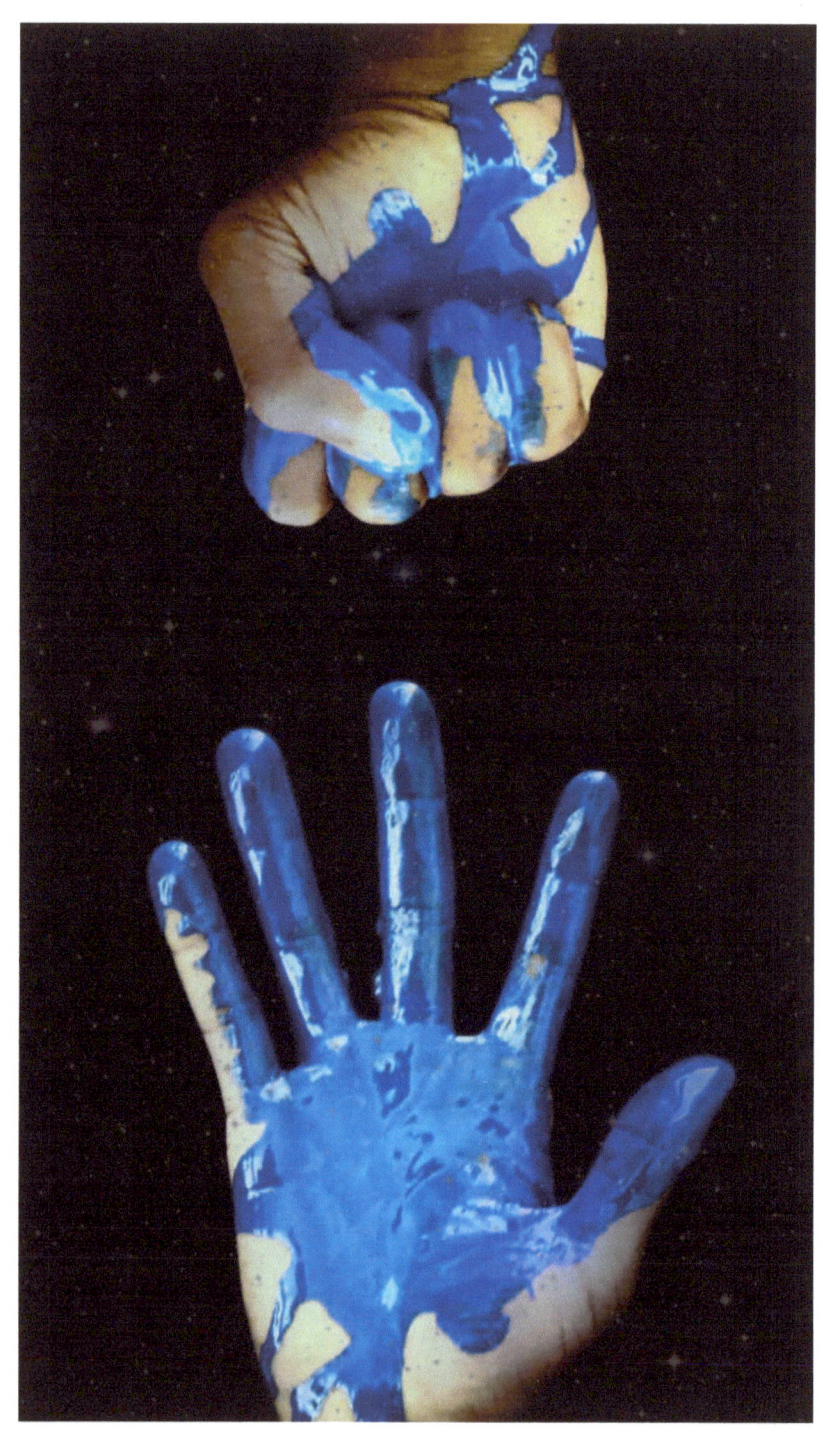

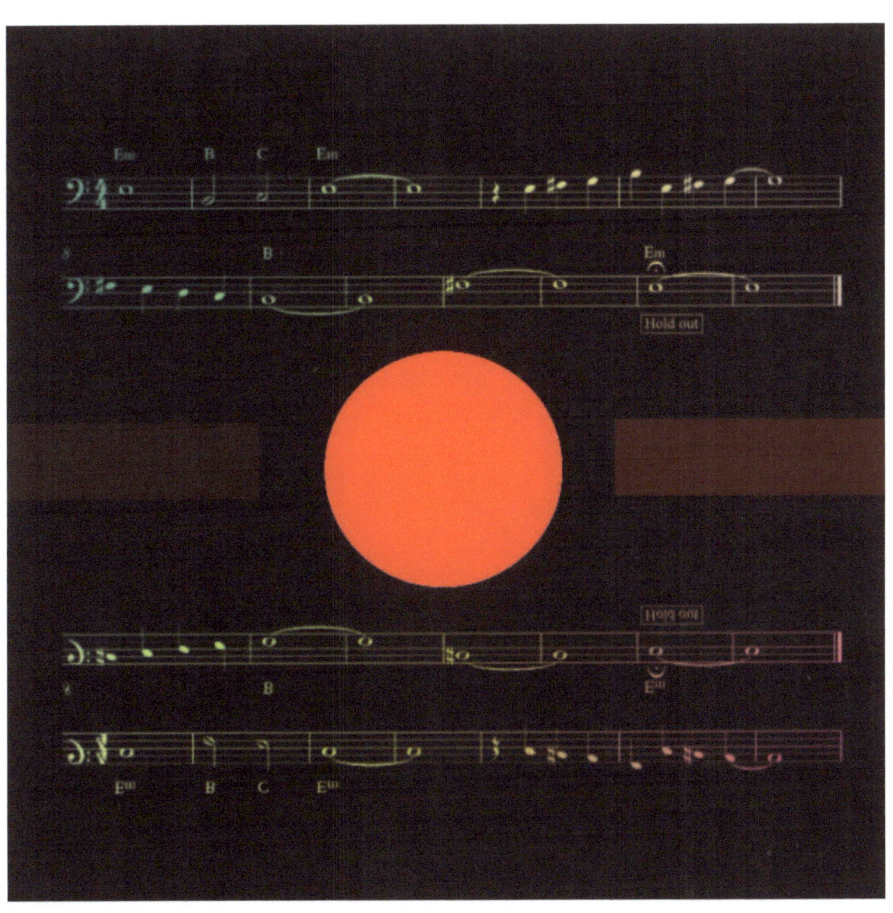

featured artists

SOPHIA of Meandsophia Photography
Pg 7-9. "finding out" photograph.
Subject, Briana Janee
Pg 39-41. "amidala the phoenix" photograph.
Subject, Avion Lopez
Pg 71-73. "golden" photograph.
Subject, Raych Jackson

Visual Thought
Pg 11. "ode to lonely" photograph.
Subject, Justin Sky
Pg 31. "deafinite" photograph.
Subject, Justin Sky

Patrick Howard
Pg 43. "who am i v1" acrylic, aerosol on wood
Pg 99. "truth" acrylic on canvas

Jasmine Baker
Pg 69. "shores" acrylic, watercolor on canvas

AZUL

Pg 25. "Broken Cosmic Course"
for reality's remorse.
Acrylic, oil, aerosol on wood
Pg 67. "As I Drown/Pull Me to the Sky"
for shores.
Acrylic, oil, aerosol on wood

Vanessa Rivera

Pg 97. "Wholeness (2016)"
for phoenix ascending, a story of love.
Acrylic and oil on wood, resin finish.

Justin Sky

Pg 15. "higher water" photograph, graphic design
Pg 37. "kamil" graphic design
Pg 47. "transitions" photograph, graphic design
Pg 61. "the end" photograph, graphic design
Pg 75. "currency" acrylic on canvas
Pg 101-103. "interview with a deity" acrylic on canvas, photography, graphic design

meandsophia.vsco.com
visualthoughtmedia.com
patrick howard
instagram.com/azulartwork
jasmine baker
vjrivera.com
justinsky.com

Thank you.

Justin Sky was born in Athens, Greece. He grew up in Victorville, California; a desert outside of Los Angeles County. He made his first ſmark during the 2010 Dub Magazine Street Level Hip Hop competition, winning the first place prize for emcees. He has performed multiple live shows internationally, and grew as the rap artist of Los Angeles' super-group, The West Coast Get Down; performing live with musicians such as Miles Mosley, Kamasi Washington, Thundercat and Cameron Graves at venues including The Viper Room, The Piano Bar, and Sayers Club, as well as Grand Performances and The Santa Monica Twilight Series.

Sky was also chosen as one of the featured poets for Blavity's 2015 "Black History" campaign. He continues to push the envelope in creative expression in the fields of music, poetry, and visual art.

Justin Sky's artistic vision is fueled by expressing a world of encouragement, escape, and entertainment through music, writing and other mediums. He aims to give his audience outer-worldly imagery intertwined with real-world feelings and scenarios.He is highly influenced by film, poetry, classical music, and the fundamental idea that "Our lives are not our own. From womb to tomb, we are bound to others, past and present. And by each crime and every kindness, we birth our future."

www.ingramcontent.com/pod-product-compliance
Lightning Source LLC
Chambersburg PA
CBHW041805160426
43191CB00004B/60